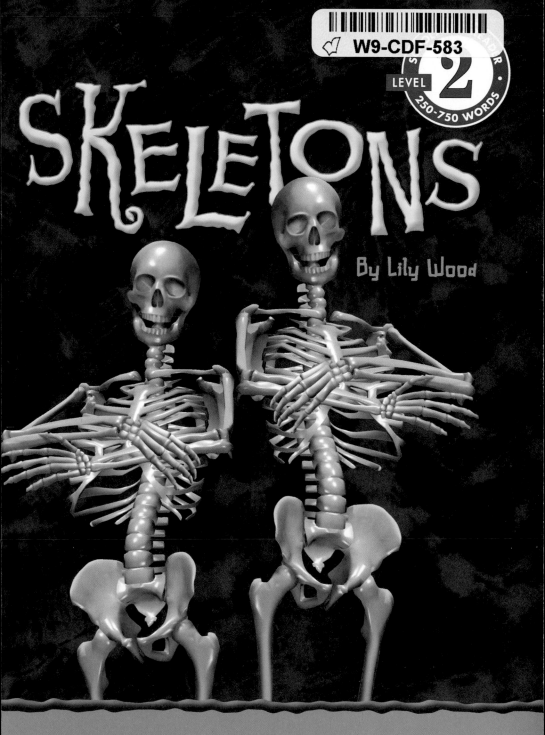

SKELETONS

By Lily Wood

SCHOLASTIC INC.
New York   Toronto   London   Sydney
Auckland   Mexico City   New Delhi   Hong Kong

Photo Credits
Front cover: © iStockphoto, inset: © Dorling Kindersley/Getty Images; Back cover: © Media
Bakery; Page 1: © iStockphoto; Page 3: © iStockphoto; Pages 4-5: © Tracy Frankel/Getty
Images; Page 7: © Media Bakery; Page 8: © ISM/Phototake; Page 11: James Stevenson/
Photo Researchers, Inc.; Page 12: © Visuals Unlimited/Corbis; Page 13: © iStockphoto;
Page 14: © Alain Pol/ISM/Phototake; Page 17: © 3D Clinic/Getty Images; Page 18: © Alain
Pol/ISM/Phototake; Page 21: © Ron Mensching/Phototake; Page 22: © pirita/Shutterstock;
Page 23: © Philip Dowell/Getty Images; Page 26: © Philip Dowell/Getty Images; Page 27:
© iStockphoto; Page 28: © Ron Menschling/Phototake; Page 29: © Medical (RF)/Photo
Researchers, Inc.; Page 30: © iStockphoto; Page 31: © iStockphoto

No part of this work may be reproduced, stored in a retrieval system,
or transmitted in any form or by any means, electronic, mechanical, photocopying,
recording, or otherwise, without written permission of the publisher.
For information regarding permission, write to Scholastic Inc.,
Attention: Permissions Department, 557 Broadway, New York, NY 10012.

ISBN 978-0-545-33148-7
Copyright © 2001, 2011 by Lily Wood
All rights reserved. Published by Scholastic Inc.
SCHOLASTIC and associated logos are trademarks and/
or registered trademarks of Scholastic Inc. Publishers since 1920.

Lexile is a registered trademark of MetaMetrics, Inc.

10 9 8 7 6 5 4 3 2 1   11 12 13 14 15

Printed in the U.S.A.   40
This edition first printing, August 2011

Your **skeleton** provides the framework of your body, like the beams of a building. It is made up of more than 200 bones.

Your muscles (muhss-uhlz) are attached to bones.

They work together to help you move. Without them, you could not run, walk, or swim!

In a museum you may see dry and white bones. Bones inside people, however, are moist and brownish or pinkish.

compact bone

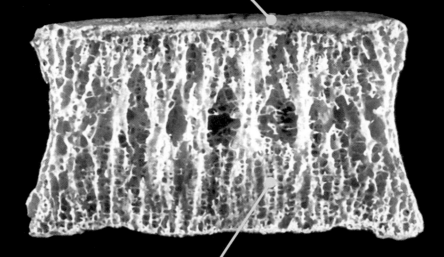

spongy bone

The hard, outer part of bone is **compact bone**. It is heavy and strong.

The inner part is **spongy bone**. Like a sponge, it has lots of spaces, which make bones fairly lightweight. Take your weight and divide by 5. That's about how much your skeleton weighs.

Ligaments attach one bone to another. Bones connect at **joints**. This allows them to move. Hinge and ball-and-socket joints are the major types of joints in your body.

Hinge joints are like doors. They allow bones to swing back and forth, but in one direction only. Your knees, elbows, and fingers have hinge joints.

The elbow is a hinge joint.

Hips and shoulders have ball-and-socket joints. The top end of the upper leg bone is rounded, like a ball. It fits into a cup-shaped socket in your hip.

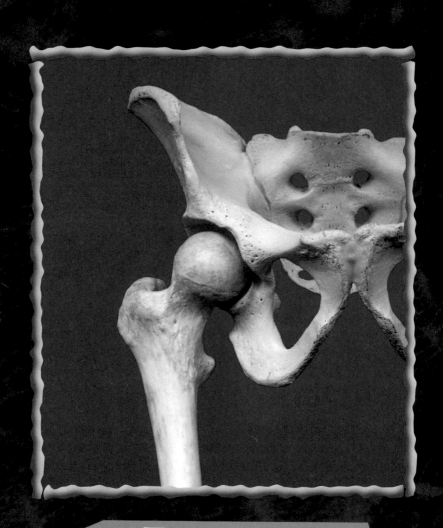

The hip is a ball-and-socket joint.

This allows your leg to have a wider range of movement, so you can run, swim, or even do a roundhouse kick.

The skull protects your brain. It's made up of 28 bones. Eight bones cover the brain, making the cranium.

Skulls look like they are missing their noses. That is because your nose is made of **cartilage**, not bone. Cartilage is tissue that is softer and more flexible than bone. It also **decomposes** faster. So skulls that you see usually have a hole where the cartilage was.

Below the skull is the spine, or backbone. It supports your body. It is made up of small bones, called vertebrae (vur-tuh-bray). Vertebrae are strung on your spinal cord— a ropelike bundle of nerves—like beads on a necklace. In between vertebrae are cushions of cartilage called discs.

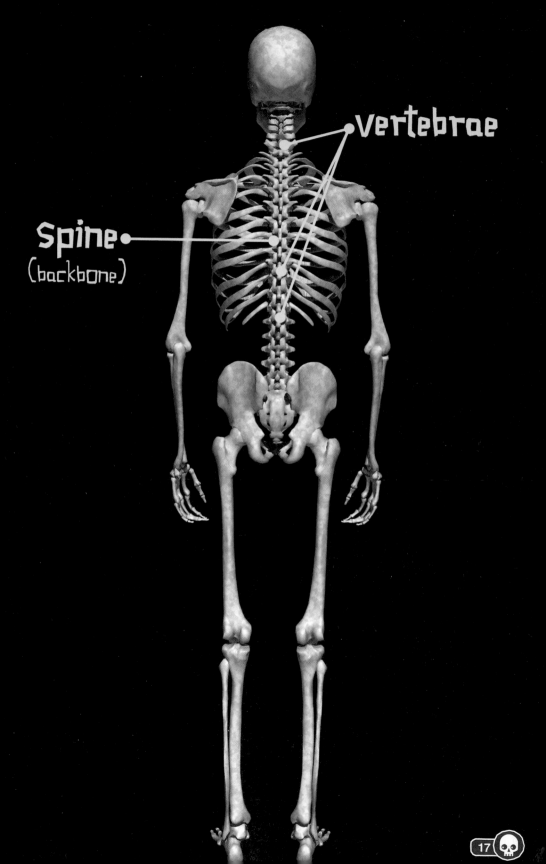

vertebrae

Spine
(backbone)

vertebrae

hip bones

Your skeleton has 33 vertebrae. The lower ones form the sacrum and the tailbone. There is a bowl-shaped collection of bones, between your hips, called the bony pelvis. It protects the organs in your lower abdomen and pelvis.

Your heart and lungs are protected by your rib cage. The rib cage is made of 12 pairs of ribs. Ribs are narrow bones that curve from your spine to the front of your chest.

Most ribs are attached to the breastbone with cartilage. This allows them to move as you breathe.

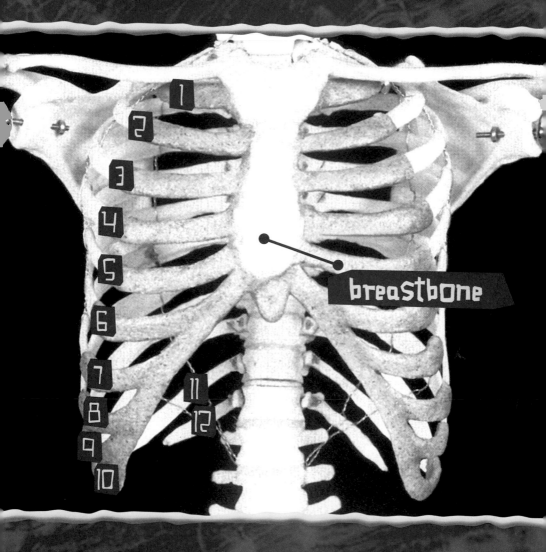

breastbone

If you raise your arms, you are using your scapulas (ska-pyoo-luhz), or shoulder blades. Your scapula connects with your upper arm bone, called the humerus (hyoo-mur-uhss).

At the elbow, the humerus attaches to two bones: the radius (ray-dee-uhs) and the ulna. They make up your forearm.

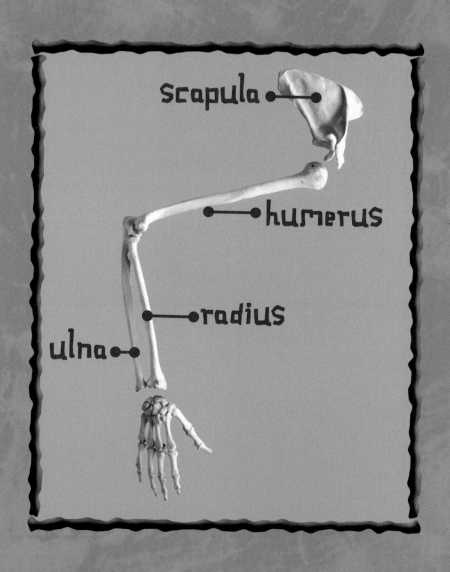

scapula

humerus

radius

ulna

Twenty-seven bones make up your hand. Your fingers are made of bones called phalanges (fuh-lan-jezz).

The 5 bones that make your palm are called metacarpals (met-uh-car-puhlz). And 8 tiny bones, called carpals, form the wrist.

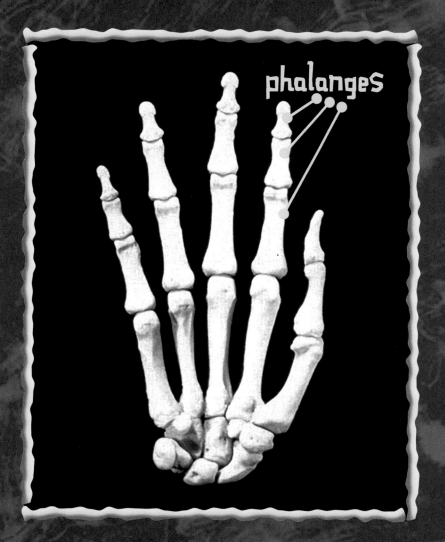

phalanges

The longest, heaviest, and strongest bone is the thigh bone, or femur (fee-mur). It has to be strong because it carries most of your weight when you are upright.

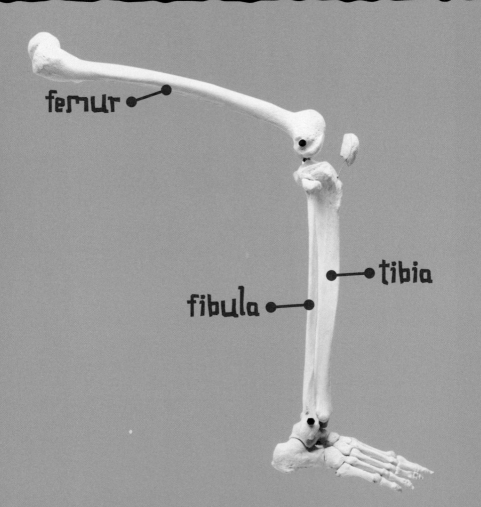

femur

tibia

fibula

The lower leg is made up of a thin bone called the fibula (fib-yoo-luh) and another large bone called the tibia (ti-bee-uh). The tibia also carries much of your weight.

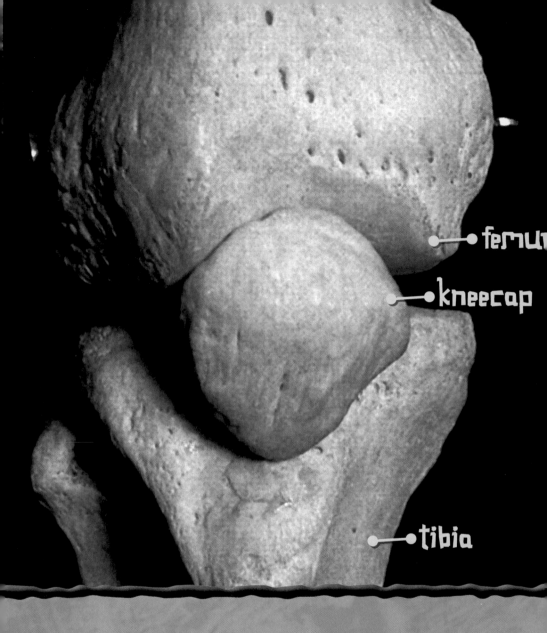

femur

kneecap

tibia

Your kneecap is not connected directly to other bones. It is set inside a **tendon.** Tendons attach muscles to bones in many parts of your body.

Your foot is made up of 26 small bones. Like your fingers, the bones in your toes are also called phalanges. These phalanges are shock absorbers, which cushion the weight of your body at every step. They also help you balance when you move.

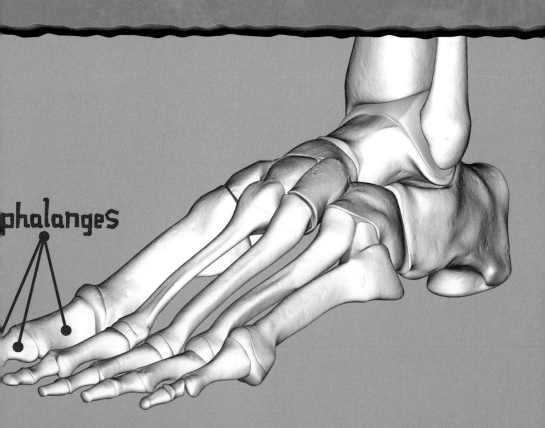

phalanges

Bones are tough, but they can break, or **fracture**. Fortunately, broken bones can heal. Take care of your bones by eating healthy and exercising.

Exercise helps build strong bones. As muscles pull on bones, the bones react by growing stronger. So to take care of your bones, keep them moving. If you take care of your bones, they'll take care of you.

Glossary

Cartilage—a tough, elastic tissue that makes up the ears and nose

Compact bone—a type of tissue that forms the hard outside of bones

Decompose—to rot or decay

Fracture—a break, such as in a broken bone

Joints—places where two or more bones meet

Ligaments—the thick, strong tissue that connects bones to one another

Skeleton—the structure that supports a body

Spongy bone—the light tissue, full of spaces, that is inside bones

Tendon—a cordlike tissue that connects muscles to bones